This book

Written and compiled by Sophie
Piper
Illustrations copyright © 2008 Tina
Macnaughton
This edition copyright © 2008 Lion
Hudson

A Lion Children's Book
an imprint of
Lion Hudson plc
Wilkinson House, Jordan Hill
Road, Oxford OX2 8DR, England
www.lionhudson.com
UK ISBN 978 0 7459 6064 7
US ISBN 978 0 8254 7840 6

First edition 2008
10 9 8 7 6 5 4 3 2 1

Acknowledgments
All unattributed prayers are by
Sophie Piper and Lois Rock,
copyright © Lion Hudson.

Bible extracts are taken or adapted
from the Good News Bible,
published by The Bible
Societies/HarperCollins Publishers
Ltd, UK © American Bible Society
1966, 1971, 1976, 1992, used by
permission.

A catalogue record for this book is
available from the British Library

Typeset in 15/20 Goudy Old Style
BT
Printed and bound in China

Distributed by:
UK: Marston Book Services Ltd,
PO Box 269, Abingdon, Oxon
OX14 4YN
USA: Trafalgar Square Publishing,
814 N Franklin Street, Chicago, IL
60610
USA Christian Market: Kregel
Publications, PO Box 2607, Grand
Rapids, MI 49501

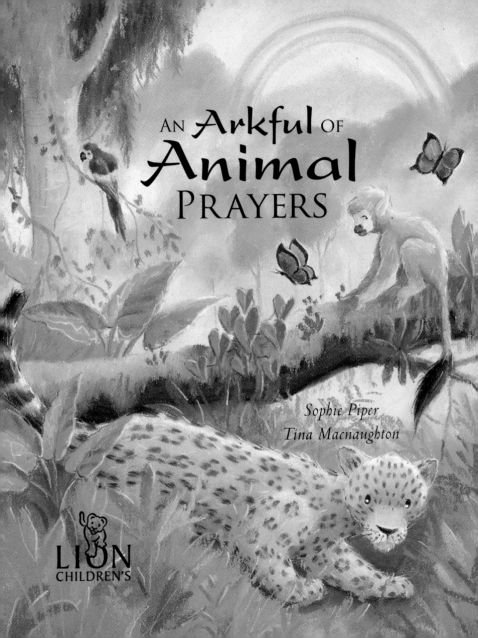

An **Arkful** OF **Animal** PRAYERS

Sophie Piper
Tina Macnaughton

LION
CHILDREN'S

'Noah,' said God, 'build me a boat
that's long and wide and sure to float.
Then search the whole world through and through,
and fetch the creatures, two by two.

'Bring them from their quiet, green places
and their lairs in wild, wide spaces.
Call the birds down from the air.
Lead the tame beasts in your care.

'Keep them quite safe from flood and rain
till all the world is clean again
when, from the olive, coos the dove,
and rainbows bend down from above.'

Contents

Quiet
green places

The little bugs that scurry,
the little beasts that creep
among the grasses and the weeds
and where the leaves are deep:
all of them were made by God
as part of God's design.
Remember that the world is theirs,
not only yours and mine.

He prayeth best, who loveth best
all things both great and small;
for the dear God who loveth us,
he made and loveth all.

S. T. Coleridge (1772–1834)

Bless our little garden. May it be a safe place
for all the little creatures that creep and
scurry through the grasses. May it be a busy
place for all the little creatures that sip and
nibble and munch among the flowers. May it
be a joyful place for all the birds that sing in
the trees.

Thank you for the food I eat –
salad leaves so fresh and sweet,
food that keeps me fit to run
and run and run and run and run.

Prayer of the rabbit

Great Maker of the leaves,
I feel myself growing tired of this world.
Tired of crawling,
tired of eating,
tired of struggling to stay alive.

Let me sleep.
Oh, let me sleep long and deep;
and then let me awaken
to a bright new world
where I can dance.

Prayer of the caterpillar

I think the butterfly
says her prayer
by simply fluttering
in the air.

I think the prayer
of the butterfly
just dances up
to God on high.

All things bright and beautiful,
all creatures great and small,
all things wise and wonderful,
the Lord God made them all.

Cecil Frances Alexander (1818–95)

God of rabbits,
God of toads,
help all creatures
cross the roads.

Save me, dear God, from the danger
that comes swooping down from the blue.
Hide me away in a small safe place
and let me keep close to you.

Prayer of the fieldmouse

Dear God,
I belong to a big colony of ants.
I expect their prayers are the same as mine.
I expect my prayers are the same as theirs.
But I am wondering –
and I expect they are all wondering the same
thing –
if you know each of us by a special name?

Prayer of the ant

I spin for myself a web of prayer
that sways to and fro in the wafting air
as God walks by in the dawning light
when heaven is almost within our sight.

Prayer of the spider

Wild wide spaces

I think of the diverse majesty
of all of the creatures on earth –
some with the power to terrify
and others that only bring mirth.
I think of their shapes and their colours,
their secret and curious ways
and my heart seems to long for a language
to sing their great Maker's praise.

Dear God,
I sometimes think I would have preferred
a stripey coat.

Other times, I think life would be simpler
if you had made me plain.

But you made me with spots and, on
reflection, there's nothing I really want
to change.

Prayer of the leopard

Help us, dear God,
to learn from all wild things.
How to live in harmony with our land;
how to deal with enemies;
how to live in peace with those who are
unlike us;
how strong is the love of a parent;
how the young must learn to grow up;
how to enjoy the beauty of strength and life
and how to accept death.

Dear God,
There are some who argue that we zebras are black animals with white stripes, while others say we are white animals with black stripes. Help us to agree that, whatever the answer, we need to stand together as a herd so that our stripes blend and we are safe together.

Prayer of the zebra

Dear God,
Make my life outstanding.

Prayer of the giraffe

O God,
All I get is abuse.
People treat me as rubbish
because I pick up theirs.
I'm not proud.
I accept the job you've given me.
But a few scraps of praise wouldn't go amiss.

Prayer of the vulture

All things bright and beautiful,
all creatures great and small,
all weevils, worms and warthogs,
the Lord God made them all.

No one can get any lower than me, O God,
and no one is more hated;
yet I have slithered into your presence
and you have not sent me away.

Prayer of the snake

I thank you, God, that I am not like other animals:

not bone-thin, like the gazelle,
not towering tall, like the giraffe,
not noisy, like the gibbering monkeys.

I am glad that you have made me squat and round and heavy so I can float at ease in the cool water and wallow in the oozing mud.

Yet, for all that, I am not always perfect.

God have mercy on me, a hippopotamus.

Prayer of the hippopotamus

Dear God,
I am weary of hunting.
I am tired of killing.
I want only to lie down
in the scorching afternoon heat
and dream of the time
when you will take your place
as king of the beasts
and everywhere is peace.

Prayer of the lion

Jesus said,
'Love your enemies;
pray for those who try to harm you.'

O God,
I will hold on to what I believe in
even if it is a tree that stands by itself.

Prayer of the koala

O God,
I came into this world with nothing
and there is no pocket deep enough
for me to take anything away.

Prayer of the kangaroo

I thought I had strength enough
never to be afraid.

But the glaciers are melting
and icebergs topple in the sea;
the waves are rising,
and the land is drowned and gone.

May God be my strength and my refuge.

Prayer of the polar bear,
based on Psalm 46

I am howling in the night, dear God;
howling alone,
howling aloud,
howling long, lonely howls
until I know that you have heard me.

Prayer of the wolf

When I lie down, I go to sleep in peace;
you alone, O Lord, keep me perfectly safe.

A prayer from the Bible, Psalm 4

Have you heard the choir of all God's
creatures –
the operatic whale
and the slightly off-key buffalo;
the timid, squeaky-voiced mouse
and the clear carolling of the blackbird?

Listen carefully:
listen for the high notes and the low notes,
for the solo and the chorus,
for the melody and the rhythm,
for the songs of love and the songs of war.

Listen for the song of all creation
in praise of the creator.

Consider
the birds

If you have heard
the sound of birdsong
in the morning air,
then you will know
that heaven's music
reaches everywhere.

This is our woodland cathedral: a blue dome of a summer sky resting on a tracery of branches, where we can sing our carols as the breeze blows invisibly by.

Prayer of the songbirds

The kingdom of God
is like a tree
growing through all eternity.

In its branches, birds may nest;
in its shade we all may rest.

O God,
Hear our cry.
The dark and cold are drawing near
and we are searching for a new homeland.
The way is long
and we grow weary
but will you,
O God,
please guide us.

Prayer of the wild geese

When I see the birds go soaring,
wheeling, dipping through the sky,
deep inside my spirit longs
to learn to fly.

God bless the birds of springtime
that twitter in the trees
and flutter in the hedgerows
and soar upon the breeze.

God bless the birds of summer
that gather on the shore
and glide above the ocean
where breakers crash and roar.

God bless the birds of autumn
as they prepare to fly
and fill the damp and chilly air
with wild and haunting cry.

God bless the birds of winter
that hop across the snow
and peck the fallen seeds and fruits
of summer long ago.

Animals around us

Dear God,
We pray for the gentle creatures who have
allowed us to tame them.
We thank you for their strength and humility.
May we be worthy of their trust.

Dear God,
May I help my dog
to grow in dogginess.
May my dog help me
to grow in humanity.

O God,
Make me a faithful
follower.

Prayer of the dog

46

Dear God,
The good I do
I will do in secret
so that not even my best friends
know about it.

Prayer of the cat

Dear God, you are my shepherd,
you give me all I need,
you take me where the grass grows green
and I can safely feed.

You take me where the water
is quiet and cool and clear;
and there I rest and know I'm safe
for you are always near.

From Psalm 23

Dear God,
There are many who are overburdened with
all the troubles of life.
May it be my privilege to help them.

Prayer of the donkey

Like the ox that ploughs so straight
with slow and steady plod,
may I learn the humble ways
to live as pleases God.

Bright
new world

Our world is fallen
as if from heaven.

Our world is broken
and we shall mend it.

Our world is wounded
so we shall heal it.

Our world is the Lord's,
and God will bless it.

Lord of the ocean,
Lord of the sea:
let all the fish swim
strong and free.

Lord of the wavetops,
Lord of the shore:
keep them all safe
for evermore.

Where the earth is ripped and torn
weave a web of green,
and add a patch of flowers so
the mend cannot be seen.

I plant a tree for the earth.
I plant a tree for the air.
I plant a tree for the whole wide world
that God gave us all to share.

God of Noah,
who sent the flood:
help us to clean the earth of all that pollutes it.

God of Noah,
who sent the rainbow:
restore the pattern of the seasons,
that there may be summer and winter
and seedtime and harvest.

God of Noah:
keep us safe in the ark of your love.
May we have faith to keep us from sinking,
hope for a better tomorrow
and love for all that you have made.

Inspired by Genesis 7–8

List of prayers by animal

Index of first lines